History in Evidence

VICTORIAN BRITAIN

Tony D. Triggs

Wayland

History in Evidence

Medieval Britain

Norman Britain

Prehistoric Britain

Roman Britain

Saxon Britain

Tudor Britain

Victorian Britain

Viking Britain

Cover design: Alison Anholt-White
Series design: Helen White
Consultant: Dr Margaret L Faull

Cover pictures: The main picture is the billiards room of Lanhydrock House in Cornwall. The wax bride doll can be seen at Kirkstall Abbey Museum, Leeds.

First published in 1990 by
Wayland (Publishers) Limited
61 Western Road, Hove
East Sussex BN3 1JD, England

British Library Cataloguing in Publication Data
Triggs, Tony D.
 Victorian Britain.
 1. Great Britain, 1837–1901
 I. Title II. Series
 941.081

HARDBACK ISBN 1–85210–582–8

PAPERBACK ISBN 0–7502–0546–6

Edited and typeset by Kudos, Hove, East Sussex
Printed in Italy by G. Canale & C.S.p.A., Turin
Bound in France by A.G.M.

Picture acknowledgements
The publishers wish to thank the following for permission to reproduce their illustrations on the pages mentioned: Chapel Studios Picture Library 10 (upper); C M Dixon 15 (upper); English Heritage 6 (lower); ET Archives 27; Mary Evans Picture Library 5, 8 (upper), 23 (upper); Kudos 7, 11, 18; Billie Love Collection 9; Mansell 16, 29 (upper), National Trust *cover* (main picture), 8 (lower), 12, 13 (both), 16, 26 (left); Skyscan 6 (upper); TOPHAM 10 (lower), 14, 15, (lower), 19 (upper), 20 (lower), 21, 22, 23, (lower), 25, 28, 29 (lower), 30; Derek Widdicombe *cover* (inset), 22 (lower: Colin Westwood), 20 (upper), 26 (right); Yorkshire Mining Museum 24. The artwork on page 4 was provided by Malcolm S Walker.

Contents

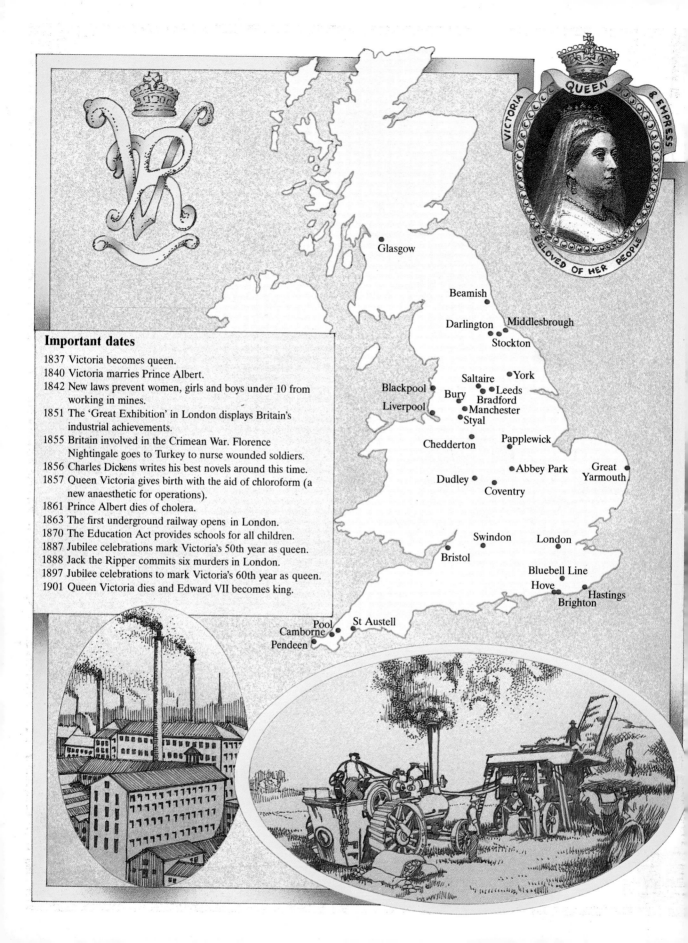

Important dates

1837 Victoria becomes queen.

1840 Victoria marries Prince Albert.

1842 New laws prevent women, girls and boys under 10 from working in mines.

1851 The 'Great Exhibition' in London displays Britain's industrial achievements.

1855 Britain involved in the Crimean War. Florence Nightingale goes to Turkey to nurse wounded soldiers.

1856 Charles Dickens writes his best novels around this time.

1857 Queen Victoria gives birth with the aid of chloroform (a new anaesthetic for operations).

1861 Prince Albert dies of cholera.

1863 The first underground railway opens in London.

1870 The Education Act provides schools for all children.

1887 Jubilee celebrations mark Victoria's 50th year as queen.

1888 Jack the Ripper commits six murders in London.

1897 Jubilee celebrations to mark Victoria's 60th year as queen.

1901 Queen Victoria dies and Edward VII becomes king.

VICTORIA QUEEN & EMPRESS
BELOVED OF HER PEOPLE

Glasgow

Beamish

Darlington Middlesbrough
Stockton

Saltaire York
Blackpool Bury Leeds
Liverpool Bradford
Manchester
Styal

Chedderton Papplewick

Abbey Park Great Yarmouth
Dudley
Coventry

Swindon London
Bristol
Bluebell Line
Hove Hastings
Brighton

Pool St Austell
Camborne
Pendeen

Victorian times

Queen Victoria reigned from 1837 to 1901, and Britain went through many changes during this time. In 1837 most people lived in villages and worked on the land; by 1901, most lived in towns and worked in offices, shops and factories. It was a time of enormous wealth and progress. New steam-powered machines (and low-paid workers) turned out cloth and other goods more cheaply than ever.

We can learn about the Victorians in various ways. For example, we can still see many of their buildings. Enormous Victorian railway stations remind us that rail was a new and important form of transport, and the banks that were built in Victoria's reign remind us that some Victorians made a great deal of money. We can also study Victorian maps and documents, such as forms that were filled in during censuses. A census is a check on every household, and the forms give us information about the size of families and the work they did. Libraries often have copies of these forms.

ABOVE Photography was invented early in Queen Victoria's reign. Pictures, like this one of a girl in a textile mill in Lancashire, have survived to tell us about daily life in the late 1800s.

OPPOSITE All the places mentioned in this book are shown on this map. The pictures at the bottom show textile mills in Yorkshire and a threshing machine at work, powered by a traction engine.

Photography was invented during Victoria's reign, so people could now record on film what daily life was like. Some of their photographs are kept in museums and libraries, and many appear in modern books. Museums also have all sorts of things which Victorian people made and used. These, too, help to show what life was like in Victorian times.

Public buildings

Many town halls, libraries and other public buildings date from Victorian times. Most of these buildings are very grand, which shows how proud the wealthy Victorians were of their country.

The Victorians built in all sorts of styles. However, their buildings often included arched doorways and windows, and circular columns.

ABOVE Before the Victorians, people did not have the equipment to create buildings that had large domes. This is the Albert Hall, in London. LEFT This is the outside of St Pancras Station in London. It is a good example of the type of grand buildings made by the Victorians.

Sometimes the slope of the roof made a large triangular shape above the entrance or upper windows, and the builders did their best to make this noticeable. They were trying to copy the style of earlier builders whose work they admired. They also included towers in some of their large public buildings. Often the towers had very steep roofs with fancy pinnacles on top. The British Museum of Natural History in London (built in 1880) has towers of this sort.

The Victorians did not always copy old styles of building. For example, London's Coal Exchange and Albert Hall have large, wide domes built partly of metal. It would have been extremely hard to make and transport the metal parts before the start of Victoria's reign. Domes had been built before, but never quite like these ones. The Crystal Palace was another Victorian building in London whose design depended on metal. It stood until 1937, when it was burnt down, but it can still be seen in photographs.

ABOVE Many Victorian buildings contained a lot of metal because it had become easier to make and to transport the metal parts. This is a huge metal 'greenhouse' in Kew Gardens, London, which was completed in 1899.

IS IT VICTORIAN?

If we want to check that a building is Victorian, we can look for a date on its walls. We can also check old maps, reports and photographs in a local library. Names of roads can sometimes give us useful clues. Many roads are named after Queen Victoria and her husband Albert, and where we see Victorian names, we can sometimes find Victorian buildings. Names like 'Jubilee Street' were often given in the final years of Victoria's reign, since 'jubilee' celebrations were held in 1887 and 1897 to mark her 50th and 60th years as queen. Streets were also named after the 'Great Exhibition' of British trade and industry which was held in 1851.

City slums

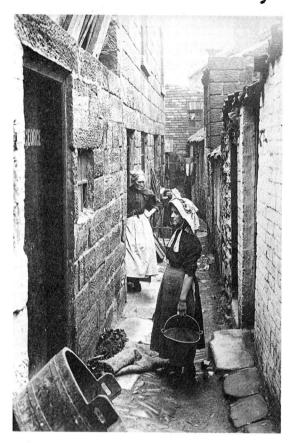

A Victorian photograph of some back-to-back houses in a Yorkshire town.

In the first half of the 1800s, factories and mills were built in many cities. The owners needed men, women and even children to work their noisy and dangerous machines, so they built houses very near their factories. At that time, there were no laws to make people build in a way that was safe for health. Piped water and toilets were rare, and some parts of cities were terribly overcrowded. Rows of workers' houses were usually built back to back with only a single room on each floor.

Sometimes two or three families had to share a house. This meant that up to eight or nine people lived and slept in each room – or perhaps in the cellar. We know about this from Victorian drawings and censuses. We also know because Members of Parliament (MPs) sometimes mentioned it in their speeches. One MP said that in Bury, Lancashire, families of up to seven people had to share a single bed in some houses.

Early in Queen Victoria's reign, a man called Edwin Chadwick pointed out that

This is Styal village, Cheshire. These buildings were once outside lavatories.

disease was harming the rich as well as the poor. It was robbing factory owners of workers; and although the owners lived in cleaner areas of the cities, it sometimes threatened *their* health too. Also, there was the cost of caring for children whose parents had died of disease.

In 1848 the government passed the first-ever Health Act which allowed councils to charge rates for work to do with public health, such as cleaning the streets and providing drinking water and underground sewers. Some cities now banned the building of back-to-back houses, and conditions slowly improved throughout Queen Victoria's reign.

Back-to-back houses can still be seen in some industrial areas, such as parts of West Yorkshire, and examples are being rebuilt in the grounds of the Bradford Industrial Museum. These will be furnished so that visitors can see what workers' living conditions were like. Most of the remaining back-to-back houses were built in the second half of Queen Victoria's reign, when streets had underground sewers and toilets. Sometimes there was a yard with several toilets which the people shared. A few of these yards have survived – for example, in Bingley, West Yorkshire – although the houses now have toilets inside.

Extract of an entry in the records for the CENSUS of SCOTLAND of   April 5th   **1891**

Held in the custody of the General Register Office for Scotland, New Register House, Edinburgh   1891/644^9/26/22

Parish or district   Kelvin   City or county   Burgh Glasgow

Note: Particulars of relationship to head of family and condition as to marriage are not included in the Returns for 1841

Road, street etc., and no. or name of house	Name and surname of each person	Relation to head of family	Condition as to marriage	Age	Rank, profession or occupation	Where born
Kent Road	James Biggar	Head	Mar	59	Managing Foreman Joiner Retired	Lanarkshire Glasgow
7 Walworth Terrace	Mary Biggar	Wife	Mar	56	.	Stirlingshire Carronshore
	Mary Biggar	Daur	Unm	32	House Keeper	Lanarkshire Glasgow
	Hugh Biggar	Son	Unm	29	Foreman Joiner	Do
	John Biggar	Son	Unm	16	Clerk	Do
	Thomas Biggar	Son	Unm	14	Office Boy	Do
	Minnie Russell	Grand Daur		9	Scholar	Do
	Bessie Russell	Grand Daur		7	Do	Do
	Annie Russell	Grand Daur		5	Do	Do
	Margaret McLean	Visitor	Unm	58	Laundress	Stirlingshire Carronshore
	Robert Biggar	Son	Unm	18	Clerk	Lanarkshire Glasgow

Given under the Seal of the General Register Office, New Register House, Edinburgh on   20th July 1978   RXO12(T)

This is the entry for one house in the 1891 census of Glasgow.

Rich and poor

The richest Victorians lived in country mansions surrounded by private parks. They had servants to prepare their meals, gardeners to look after their land and coachmen to take them out in carriages when they wanted.

In Bingley, West Yorkshire, there used to be a mansion known as Milner Fields. It was owned by a man called Titus Salt, whose father had built a nearby mill. To get to the mill, the Salt family made a drive nearly 2 km long, with a private bridge across a wide river. The mill, the drive and the site of the bridge can still be seen at Saltaire in West Yorkshire. The

ABOVE This is the textile mill built by Sir Titus Salt. It can still be seen in Saltaire, but it is no longer working.

house has gone, but books, reports and photographs tell us a great deal about it. Most Victorians got their water from wells, pumps or taps in the street, but Milner Fields had water piped from nearby springs. Its indoor toilets were also quite an unusual feature.

Most of the walls inside the house were covered in sheets of polished wood, and the doorways and beams had beautiful carvings. As well as its dining-rooms, lounges and bedrooms, Milner Fields had a billiards room, a library, a music room with an organ, and a conservatory with

ABOVE People still live in the houses in Saltaire, West Yorkshire, which were built by Sir Titus Salt for the workers in his mill. The houses were better than most workers' homes.

This row of houses in Hove, East Sussex, was completed in 1860. The houses were the seaside homes of rich people. Compare them to the workers' homes in Saltaire.

vines, birds and marble statues. Members of Queen Victoria's family sometimes stayed at Milner Fields, and they probably thought it was just like a palace!

Milner Fields was very different to the homes in Saltaire. Sir Titus Salt's father built this village to house his workers. Some of its houses were larger than others, to match the workers' different positions in the factory. However, all of them were tiny compared to Milner Fields, and censuses show that up to eight or nine people lived in some of them.

The homes in Saltaire were better than workers' homes in other parts of Britain. This was because Sir Titus Salt had the workers' health and welfare in mind when he built the village. He provided all the things he believed they needed – such as churches and other public buildings – and none of the things he thought were bad – such as public houses. Most of the buildings are still in use, although the mill itself has now closed down.

Inside houses

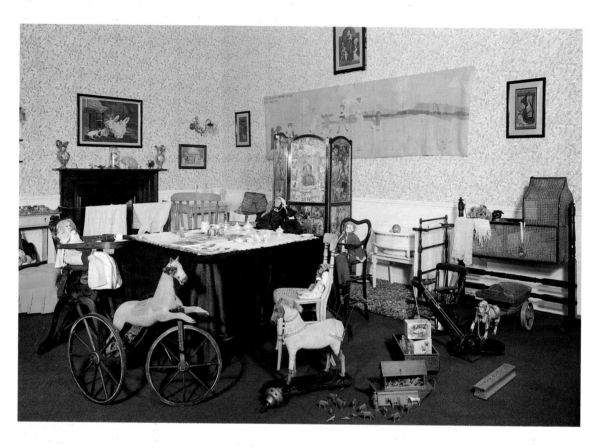

This is the nursery of Wallington House, in Northumberland, with some of the toys you would have found in the home of a rich family.

The Victorians often filled their rooms with furniture and ornaments. The furniture was made of leather and dark-coloured wood. This, and the use of dark red and dark brown paint, made the rooms seem rather gloomy. Victorian rooms were especially gloomy after dark. Electric power was being introduced at the end of Victoria's reign, but mainly for things like electric trams.

Homes had none of the electrical goods we take for granted nowadays. Radio and television had not been invented, and even electric lights were unknown. Instead, the Victorians lit their downstairs rooms with gas lamps, which were rarely as bright as modern bulbs. Some streets were also lit by gas, and a man used to go round the streets at night and light up the lamps. You can see Victorian gas lamps at

This kitchen range can be seen at Erdigg House, in Clwyd. Notice the 'copper' (to the left of the range) for heating water.

privacy and to keep themselves warm.

Many Victorian homes had maids, who lived in basement or attic rooms and did most of the chores. Being a maid or a servant was probably better than having to work in a factory and live in a slum. However, some maids did not have enough to eat, and a few died from overwork and exhaustion.

Maids and the women of poor families had to wash clothes by hand. Sometimes clothes were scrubbed on a special rough board, called a scrubbing board. Others went into a 'dolly tub', where women pounded them with a stick, called a 'dolly', from which the tub got its name. All these things can be seen in museums, such as the North of England Open Air Museum at Beamish Hall, in County Durham.

the Abbey House Museum in Leeds.

Few homes had gas lamps upstairs, so Victorians had to take candles when they went to bed. Poor people had to use candles for all their lighting, especially at the start of Victoria's reign.

Most Victorian kitchens had a range. This was a heavy iron oven and hob which were heated by a blazing fire. When people wanted a lot of hot water, they sometimes heated it up in a metal tub (a 'copper') which had its own fire underneath. Most families had a metal bath which they placed in front of the kitchen range and filled from the copper. Sometimes they put a screen around it for

Here is some of the laundry equipment used by a wealthy family's maids to wash clothes. A 'dolly tub' is on the left. (A 'dolly' is the stick used for pounding the clothes in the tub.)

Potteries and mines

We can still see the remains of Victorian industries – such as factories and mines. In earlier times, mines had often been forced to close because rain kept flooding them. Early in the 1700s, a man called Thomas Newcomen had designed a pump to get rid of the water. Newcomen's pump was driven by steam from a coal-fired boiler. Although it did not work very well, the use of steam was a very important new idea. During the 1800s, the power of steam was used to work all sorts of machines, such as spinning and weaving machines in factories, pumps in mines and locomotives on the new railways. The Geevor Tin Mining Museum (see page 30) has all sorts of engines and other equipment from local mines, and engines can also be viewed at Pool, near Redruth in Cornwall. Several old mines can be seen in the area, and some have Victorian engine houses and other buildings.

ABOVE Narrow boats, like this one, were once used on canals to carry 'china clay' from Cornwall to the potteries in Staffordshire.

The area near St Austell, in Cornwall, also shows the effects of Victorian industry. Here, we can see how clay works have covered the countryside with hillocks and pits. The clay is known as 'china clay', and was used for making fine white china. The workers uncovered the clay by removing a layer of soil; then they let a stream of water wash it out of the ground or turn it into a sloppy 'cream' which they pumped up with the help of their engines. There was often a lot of grit in the clay and the workers dumped it around the site, forming the hillocks we see today. Some of the clay works are still in use, but one, called Wheal Martyn, is now a museum.

Much of the clay was sent by canal and sea to Staffordshire. Potters have worked there for centuries, and some of the towns

ABOVE This building houses the steam-driven pump which kept the tin mine dry at Camborne, in Cornwall.

in the area are known as the Potteries. The industry grew up in Staffordshire because the area has a lot of clay, and also plenty of coal to heat the kilns in which the pots are baked. The local clay is not as fine and white as Cornish china clay, but Staffordshire potters found that they could improve it by adding powdered flint (a sort of stone). In Staffordshire, there are several museums where visitors can see the Victorian potters' kilns and workshops. They can also visit a mill at Chedderton, near Leek, where flint was ground up. A similar mill at Thwaite Mills, in Leeds, is being turned into a museum.

ABOVE This Victorian photograph shows the finishing touches being added to a clay carving by a potter in Staffordshire.

Steam at work

This Victorian photograph shows the inside of a bicycle factory in Coventry. The belts carried power from huge steam engines to the machines.

During Queen Victoria's reign, thousands of spinning and weaving mills were built in the Midlands, northern England and southern Scotland. Nearly all of them had steam-powered machinery. At Bradford, in West Yorkshire, a Victorian mill has been turned into a museum, and visitors can sometimes see Victorian engines and machines in action. The workrooms in the mill are enormous, and each must have had about 50 workers. Belts carried the engines' power to all the machines. When all the machinery was working, the noise must have damaged the workers' ears.

In Victorian times, people did not know that noise can cause deafness. However, they knew that dirty, overcrowded conditions can cause disease. We have already seen how Sir Titus Salt (see pages 10 and 11) tried to give his workers healthy homes. Another wealthy Victorian, called Joseph Cash, built rows of homes round a central courtyard. Each row had a workshop on the top floor, and this was shared by all the people in the row. An engine in the courtyard provided the power for all the machinery, so Cash's system was cheap to run and the people lived and worked in pleasant, homely conditions. Cash's buildings, called 'Top Shops', can still be seen in Coventry.

Many new things in Victorian England depended on steam. For example, steam-powered pumps were needed at the sewage and waterworks the Victorians built. At Abbey Park, near Leicester, a Victorian sewage works has been turned into a museum, and at Kew, in London, and Papplewick, near Nottingham, the same has been done with waterworks. The Victorians were proud of their sewage and waterworks, since they helped to turn their cities into healthy places. At Papplewick, they showed their pride by decorating the inside of the pumping station with all sorts of wildlife designs.

At Styal in Cheshire, there is a museum where you can see all the weaving machinery that was once used in a textile mill. Steam engines provided the power for the machines.

Railways

Until the start of Victoria's reign, most people made their journeys on foot, and they rarely travelled far from their homes. Those who wished to make longer journeys usually went on horseback, by horse-drawn coach or by sea. Travel was hard because the roads were poor, and coaches and carts often sank into the mud after heavy rain. However, during Queen Victoria's reign, travel became much easier. The change had begun in the 1820s, with the opening of railways from Stockton to Darlington and Liverpool to Manchester. Other railways were opened during the 1830s and 1840s.

Fares were low, and this meant that

On the Bluebell Line in East Sussex you can travel in Victorian railway carriages pulled by this locomotive, which was built in Glasgow in 1885.

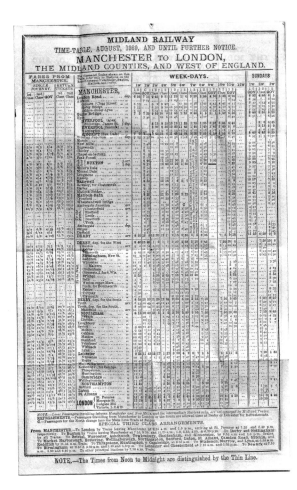

A page from the Midland Railway's timetable, published in August 1869.

The railways even affected the way people told the time. They had always set their clocks and watches by the sun. This meant that midday was slightly later in the west of the country than in the east. When people went from London to Bristol, they found that all the clocks in the city seemed to be slow. This was especially confusing for train drivers and signalmen. In the end, a standard 'railway time' was introduced across the whole of Britain. It was based on the time at Greenwich in London, and this is the time we still use today.

Lastly, the railways carried news and ideas. Previously, news had taken days to reach people outside the cities; now it came overnight.

The early trains had steam locomotives. Many of these can still be seen at the National Railway Museum in York, and others are used to pull passenger trains on railways in various parts of Britain, such as the Bluebell Railway in East Sussex.

Trains still use this Victorian viaduct, which you can see in East Sussex.

even the poor could afford to travel by train. People in towns could get to the seaside and back in a day, and resorts like Brighton, Great Yarmouth and Blackpool doubled in size within a few years.

Industrial towns grew rapidly too. Middlesbrough began to expand as soon as there was a railway to transport the things made in its factories, and Swindon grew up round a factory that made railway engines and carriages.

Farming

Farming changed in Victorian times. At first the methods were very simple. Ploughs were usually drawn by horses and men had to scatter the seed by hand. Wheat was one of the commonest crops, and workers cut it with sickles or scythes. They beat (or threshed) it with flails in order to separate the grain from the husks and the straw; then they ground the grain into flour to make bread.

At the start of Queen Victoria's reign, some farmers began to use steam-powered machines, called traction engines. These could do as much work as several horses or men. At harvest-time, they provided the power for threshing machines. Workers used forks to load the machine with the crop which they had cut. The straw and the grain then tumbled out of separate holes. The new machines meant that wealthy farmers employed fewer people, and many villagers had to leave and find work in the cities.

In some parts of Britain, the soil was too poor for growing crops. Farmers had always used this land for sheep and cattle,

ABOVE This steam-powered traction engine was used by a farmer in Victorian times to pull a plough across fields.

RIGHT This is a photograph of hop pickers on a farm in Kent in the late 1890s. The hops were sold to breweries to make beer. Many poor people from east London used to work in the hop fields in the summer. To them, it was like being on holiday because they were away from the crowded, noisy city.

You can see this Victorian dairy at Easton Farm Park, in Suffolk. The fountain kept it cool.

so they did not need the new machines. They usually milked their cows in fields, and they brought the milk home in cans that were made to fit on their backs. They used special bowls to separate the cream from the milk, then they turned the cream into butter by shaking it up in churns. Lastly, they stamped designs on the butter to show who had made it.

These dairy farmers also made cheese. Each cheese needed squeezing to make it firm, and this was done with presses. A lot of cheese and butter came from the Yorkshire Dales, and museums in Yorkshire still have some of the tools the Victorian farmers used.

Going to school

This Victorian photograph shows what a classroom looked like in a boys' school. Note that the school did not have electricity, so the rooms were lit by gas lamps.

At the start of Queen Victoria's reign, few children ever went to school. Some attended Sunday schools, which were run by churches. The Sunday schools taught reading, writing and Bible stories. However, they met only once a week, when children had their day off work. Some children were far too tired to study, and they stayed in their beds.

Parliament gradually cut the hours which younger children had to work, and some of them started going to school for half of each day. Like the Sunday schools, the schools they attended were run by churches, but the churches could not provide enough places, and other schools were opened by rich factory owners.

We can see how many children went to school if we study the forms that were filled in during censuses. In the forms for

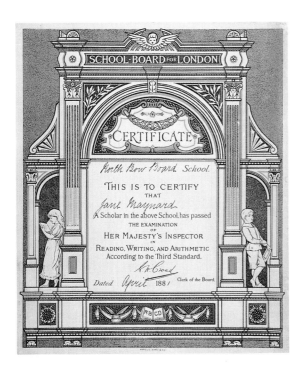

A certificate from 1881 showing that a London girl had passed her exams.

Saltaire that were completed in 1861, the word 'scholar' appears by the names of *all* the children aged from 5 to 11. This means that they were attending school. Most began work in the mill when they were 11 or 12, but some stayed at school until they were in their teens. The children in Saltaire were lucky, since the Salt family provided a school in their factory dining-room, and in 1868 they built a magnificent school which can still be seen. Census sheets for other towns and villages show that many children did not have schools in the 1860s.

At last, in 1870, Parliament passed a famous Education Act. Under this Act, towns and cities without enough schools could choose a group of people known as a School Board. The Boards had the job of starting schools and raising the money to keep them going. Soon there was room for all children under the age of 12, and Parliament said they *must* attend, whether they liked it or not. Reading and writing were now important for many jobs, and the Members of Parliament wanted to keep up a good supply of suitable workers. The 1870 Act (called the Elementary Education Act) can be consulted in most large libraries.

School was usually very dull. The children practised writing and arithmetic by scratching their work on special pieces of stone, called slates; when the slate was covered, the pupils could wipe it clean and re-use it. Classes were large, and the teacher often beat the children to make them behave. Older pupils, called monitors, helped the teachers to keep order.

Here is a group of primary schoolchildren, photographed in the late 1880s.

Child workers

During Queen Victoria's reign, workers were often treated like slaves. At the start of her reign, children had to work for up to 12 hours a day, and at coal-mines they had to crawl along narrow passages, hauling tubs of coal to the surface. The Yorkshire Mining Museum (see page 30) has life-size models of people working underground. The models are based on various clues. Old tubs, for example, have been found and some of the passages have been explored, but the most important clues are in books. Some Victorian books have pictures of children in mines, and they tell us about the work they did.

In 1842, Parliament made new laws which prevented women, and girls and boys under 10, from working in mines. However, hunger usually forced them to find new jobs in mills. The machines in the mills were dangerous as well as noisy. Children sometimes lost arms in accidents; others grew up twisted and bent because the work – like work in the mines – was too hard. One Victorian has written about a crowd of crippled children

This is a display at the Yorkshire Mining Museum which shows what conditions were like for children who worked in the mines.

A Victorian photograph showing a child working in a textile mill in Yorkshire.

outside a factory, and he said that they were bent like letters of the alphabet.

Some children worked as chimney sweeps, and to do this they had to climb up inside the chimneys. They rubbed the skin off their elbows and knees, and they sometimes swallowed a lot of soot and had trouble breathing. Most of them died of lung diseases before they grew up.

Illness, a death or unemployment could leave a family without enough money to live on. Some people starved or turned to crime; others turned to the local 'Guardians'. The Guardians collected rates and used the money to care for the poor, but they had to obey strict laws, called the Poor Laws. If sick people asked for help, they were given some money or food, but healthy people were sent to a workhouse. Conditions were as harsh as those in a prison. Families were split up, and men, women, girls and boys had to sleep in separate dormitories. They were rarely given enough to eat, and they had to do hard work, like breaking stones for roads.

Some Victorian workhouse buildings can still be seen, like the one at Keighley, West Yorkshire, and pictures and drawings show us how families were treated in these terrible places.

Shops and shopping

Today, we do most of our shopping in large shops where we can walk about and choose what we want. In Victorian times, most shops were much smaller than modern ones. Many were simply the downstairs room of the owner's home.

The picture below, on the right, shows the inside of a Victorian chemist's shop. People who could not read could pick it out because the window contained large bottles of coloured liquid. They were a sort of sign or badge, and they suggested that there was something rather old-fashioned and mysterious about the chemist's medicines. Most were obtained from plants, but the bottles and boxes all had

BELOW This is the inside of a chemist's shop. All the bottles contained medicines and many of them still have their Latin labels on. You can see the shop at the Black Country Museum in Dudley.

ABOVE This is what a Victorian shop window looked like. You can see it at Styal village, in Cheshire.

Latin names. Sometimes chemists mixed the medicines up in their shops.

We can see Victorian shops at the Abbey House Museum in Leeds, at the Black Country Museum in Dudley and at Styal village in Cheshire. The Leeds' shops are based on ones that stood in the city. They have been arranged in cobbled streets, so we can walk in and out of them just as people did in Queen Victoria's time.

Besides a grocer's and chemist's, there is an ironmonger's shop and a barber's. We can also see workshops that remind us of how important horses and carts were in Victorian times. For example, there is a workshop for making saddles and other leather goods, and another workshop for making wheels and repairing wagons. Similar streets can be seen at the Castle Museum in York.

This Victorian painting shows us what Kensington High Street, in London, looked like in 1898. Notice how little traffic there was compared to modern times, and how all the vehicles, including the buses, were pulled by horses.

Pastimes

This beautiful merry-go-round was built in the early part of Queen Victoria's reign. It is still in use today, going round Britain as part of a travelling fair. Once it was powered by a steam engine; today electricity does all the work.

Victorian children enjoyed ball games, dancing, and simple toys like marbles, tops and skipping ropes. However, teen-age and adult factory workers liked boxing, wrestling and dog-fighting, and they also enjoyed alcoholic drink, which sometimes led to rowdy behaviour. In Victorian times, the well-off people tried to discourage sports and games that were cruel or rough, and they also tried to stop people drinking too much alcohol. In their towns they set up museums, libraries, parks and zoos, where the poor could relax in a peaceful way. Parks had gates and railings and they were closed at night. This was because the Victorians felt that people should only use the park when someone was there to stop them

Books were also popular, though poorer people found reading difficult.

As we have seen, steam trains took trippers to many resorts, but the power of steam was also used to work fairground rides. At Shipley Glen, in West Yorkshire, there was a permanent fairground. One of the rides was advertised as 'The Largest, Wildest and Steepest Toboggan Slide Ever Erected on Earth.' In 1900 it closed down after a serious accident, and the other attractions have also gone. However, visitors can still ride to Shipley Glen on a Victorian tramway, and if they study the rocky ground they can see the holes where the rides were fixed.

Most Victorians also liked peaceful activities, such as boating and croquet. At Saltaire, people can still hire boats from a boathouse over 100 years old.

Day-trippers from London, brought by train, enjoying the seaside at Hastings, on the south coast, in the 1890s.

drinking alcohol or acting noisily. Parks with railings and keepers can still be seen in some towns.

In the evenings, people sometimes went to the theatre or the music-hall. They loved operettas by Gilbert and Sullivan, and these are still performed today. The Victorians also made their own music, and well-off people often had music rooms – and pianos – in their homes.

ABOVE This is modern photograph shows the clothes a Victorian woman would have worn for a game of tennis. The racquet is a copy of the type used by Victorians. Notice how it is different to today's style.

Places to visit

Abbey House Museum, Kirkstall, near
  Leeds
**Cambridge and County Folk
  Museum**, Cambridge
Canal Museum, Nottingham
Castle Museum, York
Cookworthy Museum, Kingsbridge,
  Devon
The Engineerium, Hove, East Sussex
Geevor Tin Mining Museum,
  Pendeen, near St Just, Cornwall
Gloucester Folk Museum, Gloucester
Industrial Museum, Bradford
Museum of Oxford, Oxford
**National Museum of Film,
  Photography and Television**,
  Bradford (especially the Kodak
  Museum section)
National Railway Museum, York
Nidderdale Museum, Pateley Bridge,
  North Yorkshire
North of England Open Air Museum,
  Beamish, County Durham
Papplewick Pumping Station,
  Ravenshead, Nottinghamshire
Saltaire village, near Shipley, West
  Yorkshire
Staffordshire County Museum,
  Shugborough, Staffordshire
Town Docks Museum, Hull
Wheal Martyn Museum, near St
  Austell, Cornwall
Wigan Pier, Lancashire (restored
  steam-powered mill engine)
Wollaton Park Industrial Museum,
  Nottingham
Yorkshire Mining Museum, near
  Wakefield, West Yorkshire
**Yorkshire Museum of Carriages and
  Horse-drawn Vehicles**, Aysgarth
  Falls, North Yorkshire

Most of these places are museums; it is
important to check opening times and
other details (such as when engines may
be in steam and special events) before you
go – telephone numbers will be listed in
your local phone directory. In addition,
remember that most towns and cities –
particularly London and mill towns in the
north – have some Victorian buildings.
Your local reference library will have a
local history section which may have
information on them.

Here is a collection of objects from a wealthy
Victorian family's house.

Glossary

Chores Boring jobs that have to be done every day.

Conservatory A large greenhouse built on to the side of a house. It is often used for growing plants which come from countries where the climate is hotter or for growing plants which need shelter from the wind and rain.

Crippled Having your limbs or joints damaged by a disease, an accident or by working conditions.

Harsh Very unpleasant.

Jubilee A special anniversary.

Kiln A special oven for hardening or drying pieces of pottery.

Mansion A large house with many rooms and a lot of land around it.

Monument A statue, building, etc. built in memory of a person or an event.

Operetta A short opera, usually with several funny songs and scenes in it.

Ornament Something that is used to make a room look pretty.

Pinnacle Fancy, spiky top to a tower.

Profit The extra money obtained by a business person by selling something for more than it cost to buy or make.

Range A kitchen fireplace with one or two ovens.

Raw materials Things that are needed to make something in a factory.

Rowdy Noisy, troublesome behaviour.

Thresh To beat a grain crop to get the seeds out of it.

Books to read

Chamberlin, E. *Everyday Life in the Nineteenth Century* (Macdonald Educational, 1983)

Conner, E. *A Child in Victorian London* (Wayland, 1986)

Dunning, R. *Victorian Life and Transport* (Nelson, 1981)

Harper, R. *Finding Out About Victorian Childhood* (Batsford, 1986)

Jones, M. *Finding Out About the Poor in Nineteenth-Century Britain* (Batsford, 1986)

Pollard, M. *The Victorians* (Heinemann, 1978)

Poulton, R. *Victoria: Queen of a Changing Land* (World's Work, 1975)

Rawcliffe, M. *Finding Out About Victorian Country Life* (Batsford, 1984)

Rawcliffe, M. *Finding Out About Victorian London* (Batsford, 1985)

Rawcliffe, M. *Finding Out About Victorian Public Health and Housing* (Batsford, 1987)

Rooke, P. *The Age of Dickens* (Wayland, 1971)

Ross, S. *Spotlight on the Victorians* (Wayland, 1985)

Ross, S. *A Victorian Factory Worker* (Wayland, 1985)

Sauvain, P. *A Victorian Factory Town* (Macmillan Education, 1979)

Seaman, L. *Life in Victorian London* (Batsford, 1973)

Thie, G. *The Victorians* (Blackwell, 1985)

Index

buildings 5, 6, 7

canals 15
Cash, Joseph 16-17
censuses 5, 8, 23
Chadwick, Edwin 8-9
children 8, 9, 22, 24-5, 28
china clay 15
cities 5, 8-9, 12, 19, 26
cooking 13

electricity 12

factories 8, 10, 14, 19, 23, 28
farming 5, 20-21
food 20, 21
furniture 10, 12

gas 12, 13
Great Exhibition 7
Guardians 25

health 8, 9, 16, 17, 24, 25, 26-7
housing 5, 8, 10-11, 12-13, 16-17

illness 5, 8, 9, 25
industry 5, 8, 14-15, 24

laundry 13

laws 8, 9, 23, 24, 25
leisure 28-9

mines 14, 24

Newcomen, Thomas 14

Parliament 8, 9, 22, 23, 24
Poor Laws 25
pottery 15

railways 5, 14, 18-19, 29
religion 11, 22

Salt, Sir Titus 10, 11, 16, 23
Saltaire 10-11, 23
schools 22-3
seaside 19, 29
servants 10, 13
shops 26
steam power 5, 14, 16-17, 20, 29

textile mills 10, 16, 24
traction engines 20
transport 15, 18, 27

Victoria, Queen 5, 7, 11

workhouses 25